TØ111845

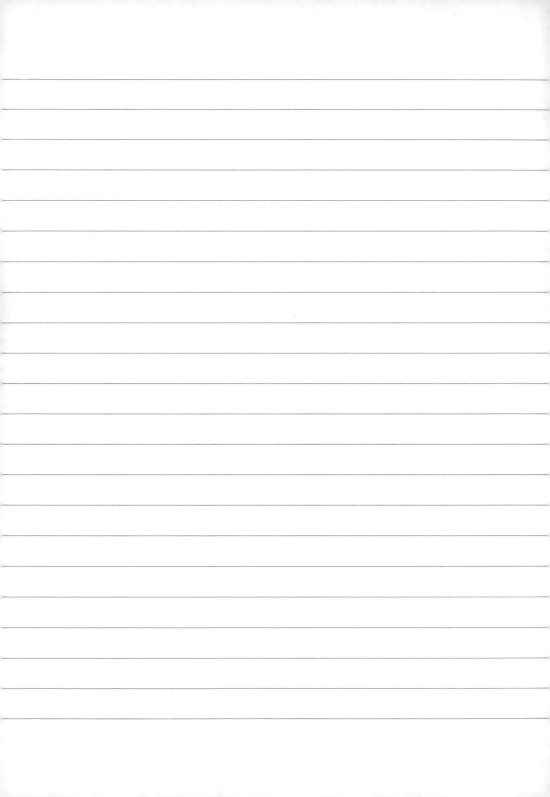

	******	******		

*****		******		

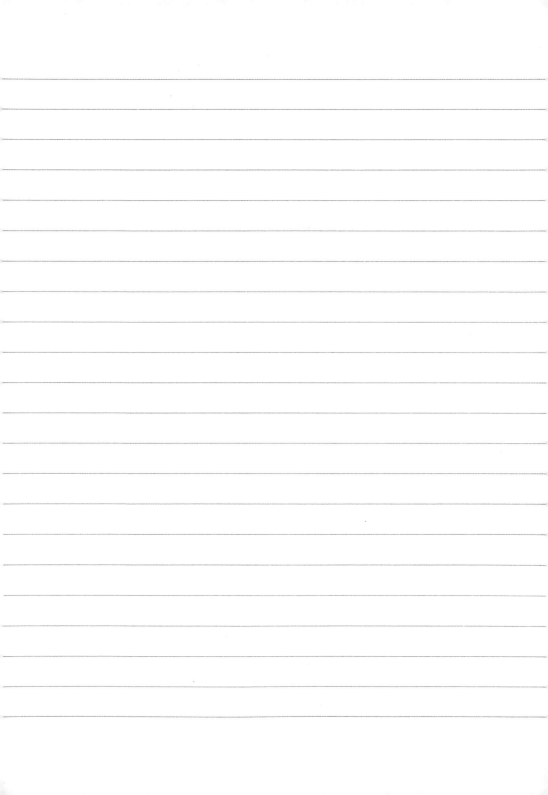

2	
<u>.</u>	

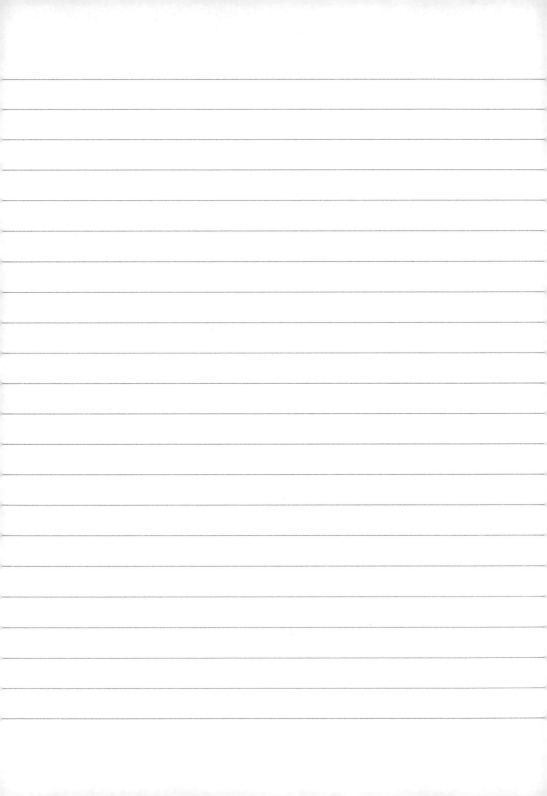

ι	

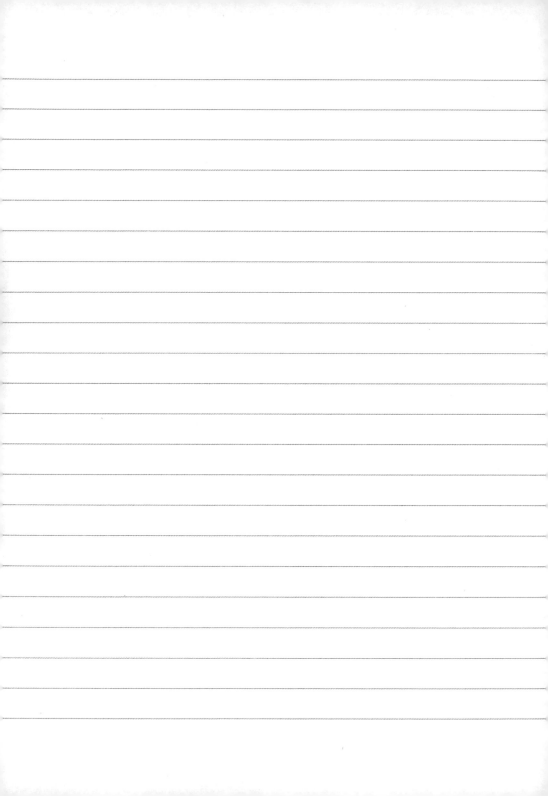

*******	 ****		

	 	******	****
>	 	******	

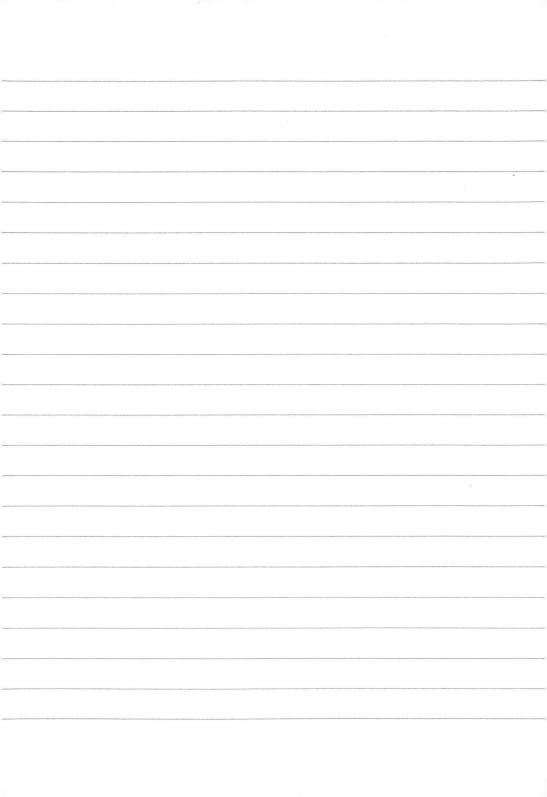

· · · · · · · · · · · · · · · · · · ·	

,				 	
	}			 	

****		****		 	

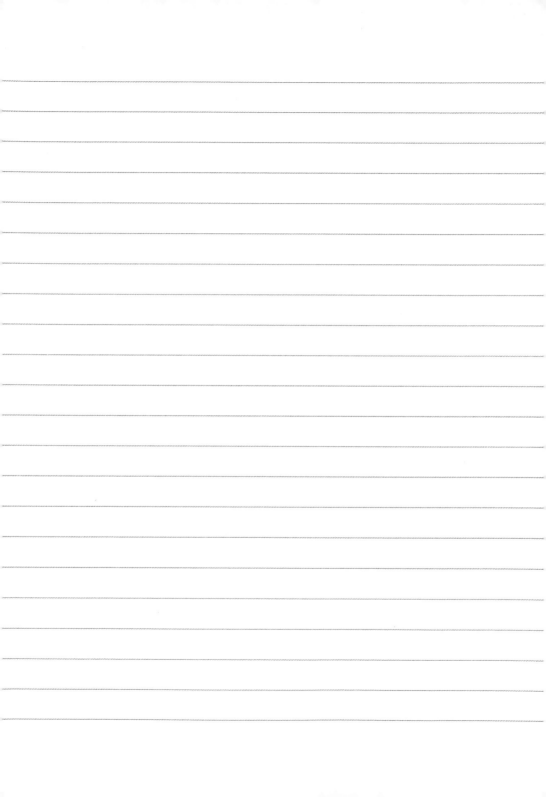

jan		
·		

	~~~~	 
\		 
)mmerer en		 

>	 		
>	 		
·····	 		
)	 		
3	 		
	 	i	

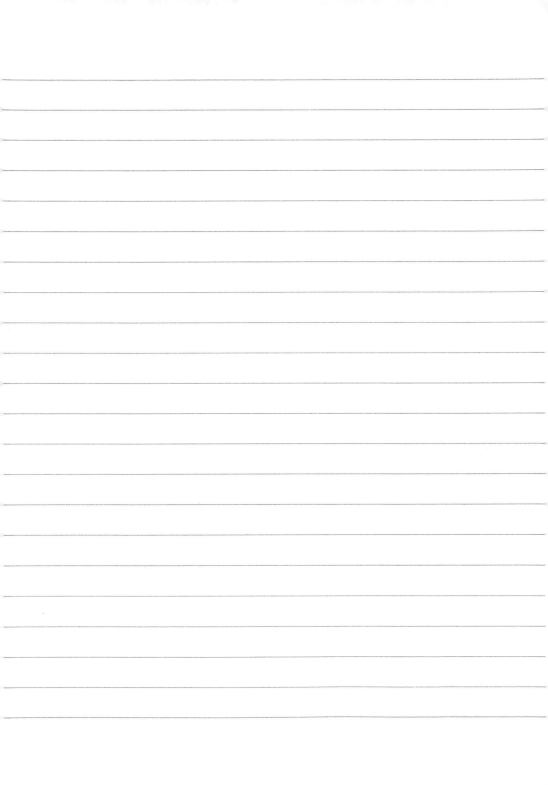

	-
· · · · · · · · · · · · · · · · · · ·	

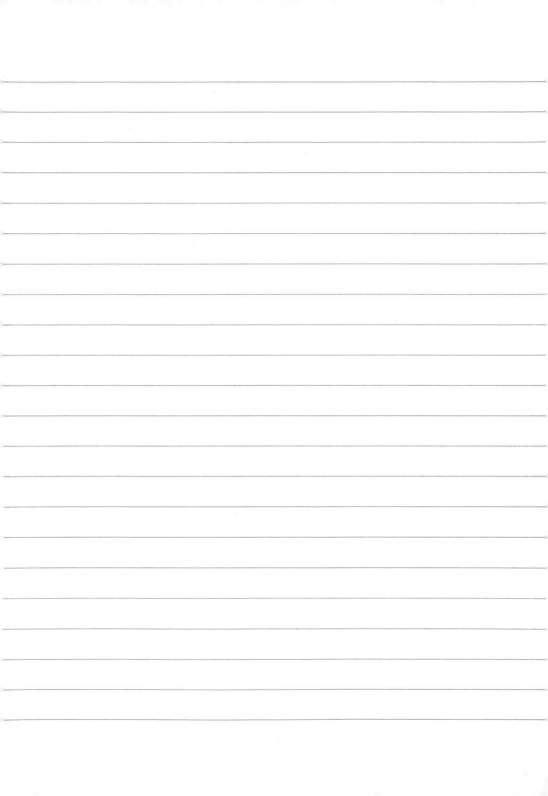

· · · · · · · · · · · · · · · · · · ·	

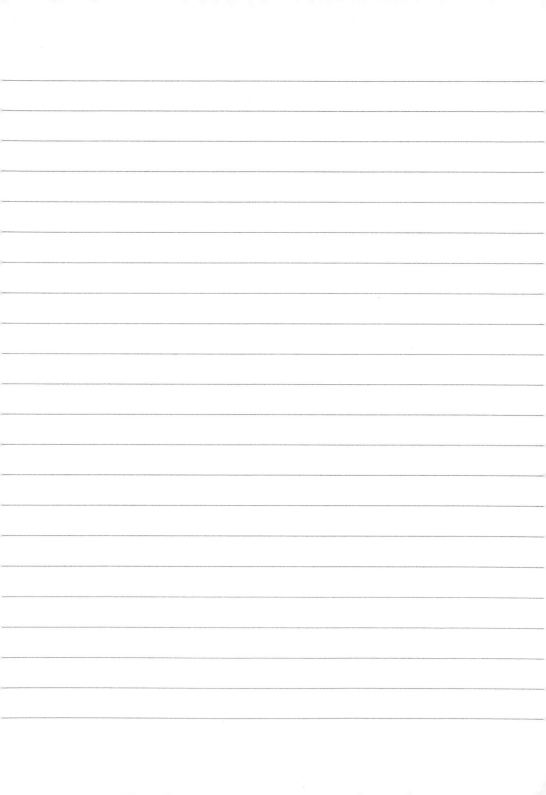

· · · · · · · · · · · · · · · · · · ·		 	
2	****	 	
heeree		 	
y			

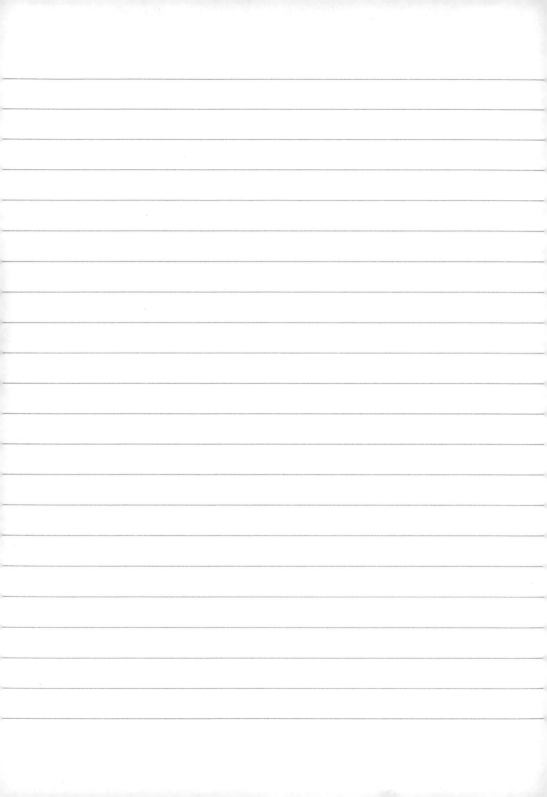


j		 	
		 *****	
·		 •	
	<u></u>	 	
·		 	
>		 	

				*****************************
***************************************				
		****		******
				****
	5			
				********
******				*****
		****		******
/				
				************************
			*****	
******				

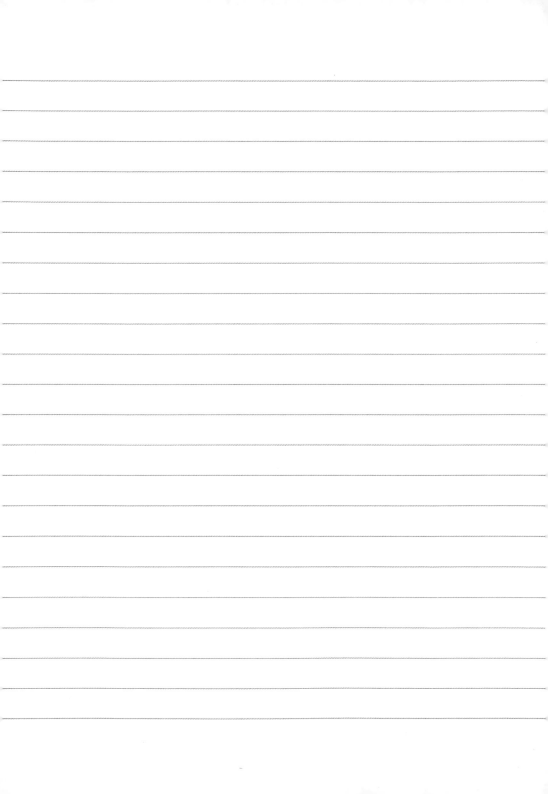

******		 	
Yerre	 	 	
·····		 	
<u></u>			

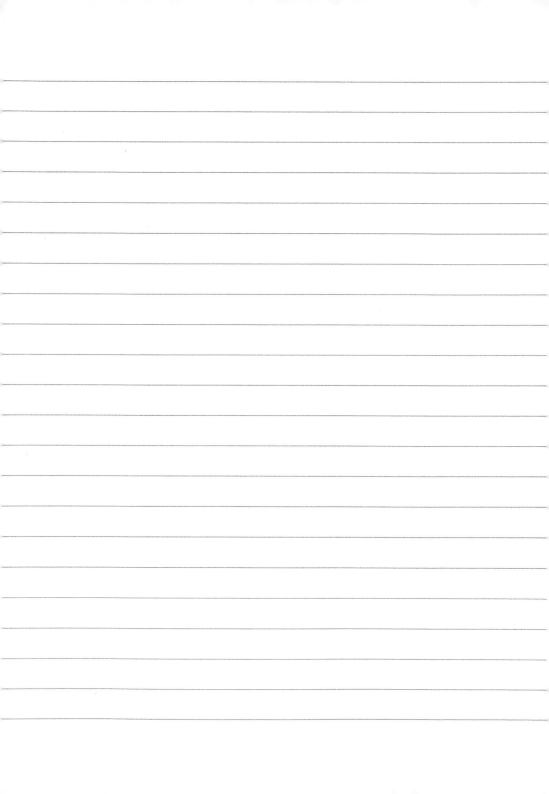

·····	- 	
·····	· · · · · · · · · · · · · · · · · · ·	

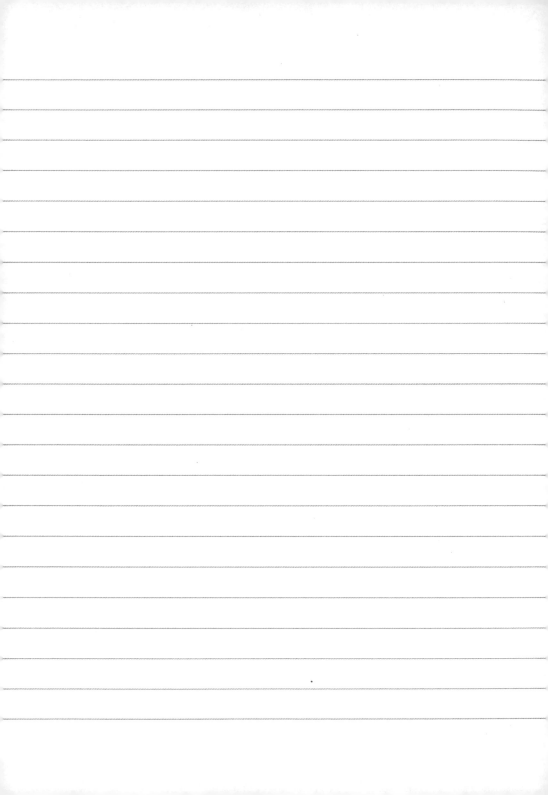

 	 	*********
 		~~~~~
 	 	•

· · · · · · · · · · · · · · · · · · ·	
· ·	

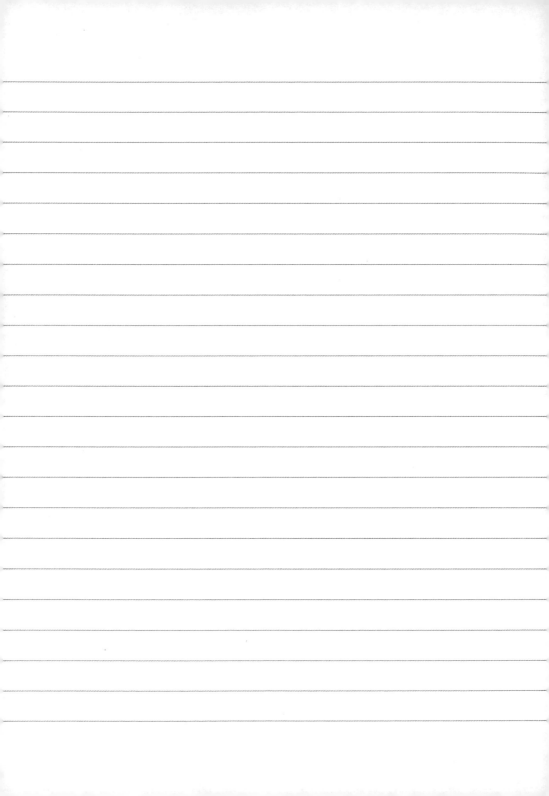

, 	

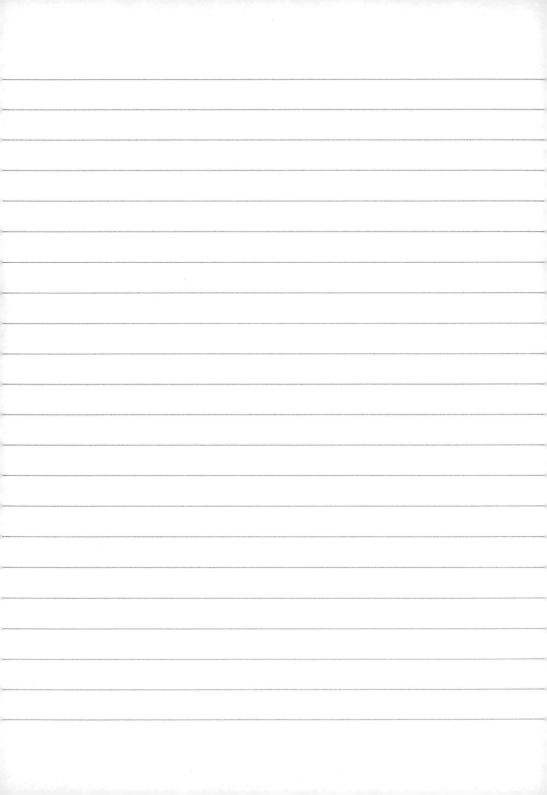

×	
>	
······	

· · · · · · · · · · · · · · · · · · ·	

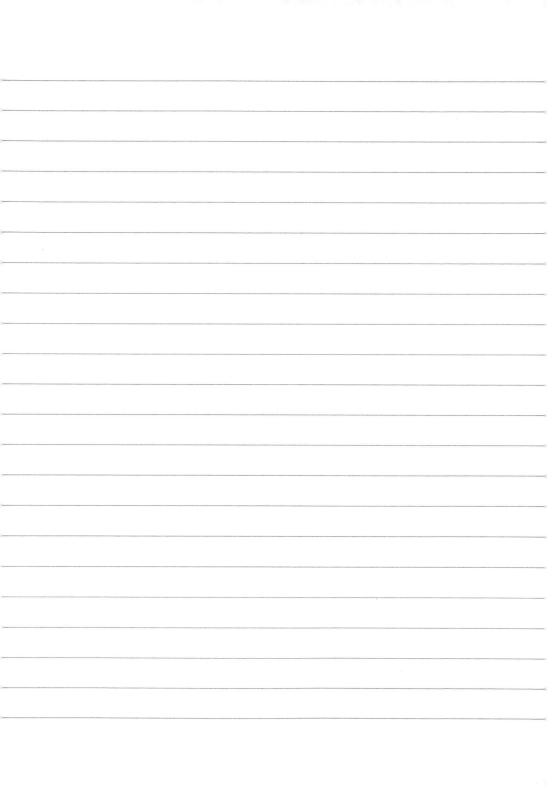

······		 	
	-	 	
	,	 	

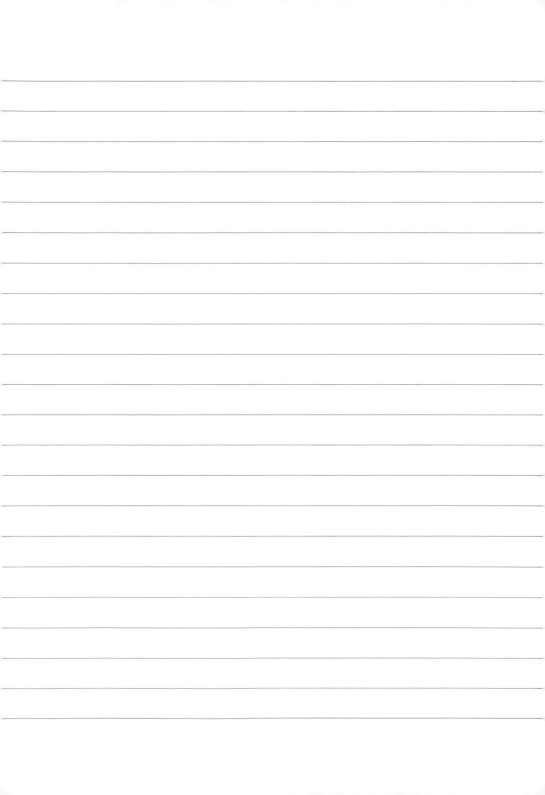

		 ****	****	 	

·····		 		 	

		 *****		 *****	****

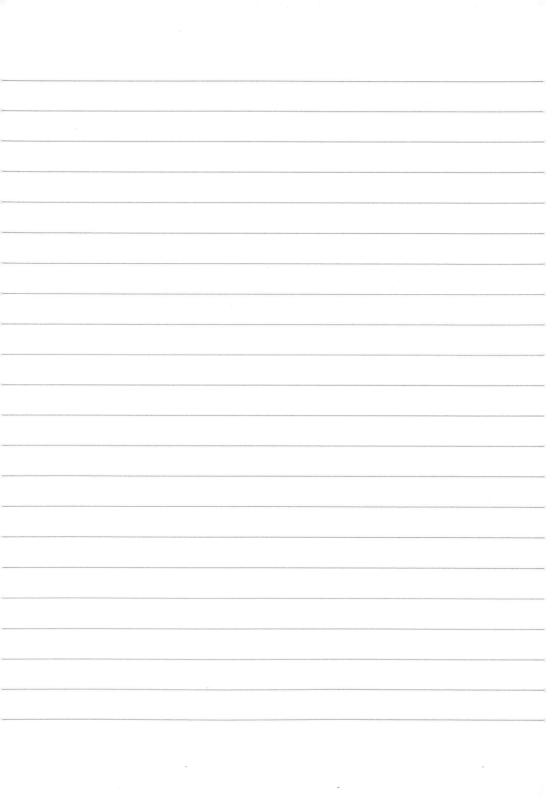

<u> </u>		 	
-	 	 	
-	 		

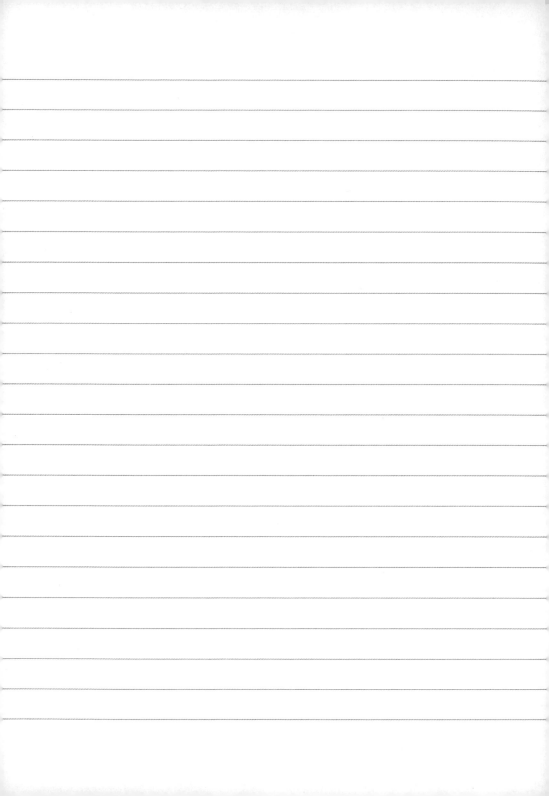

	AII NA IINA NAMA IINA NINA MAMANA MAN
·····	TØ111843
>	
	·

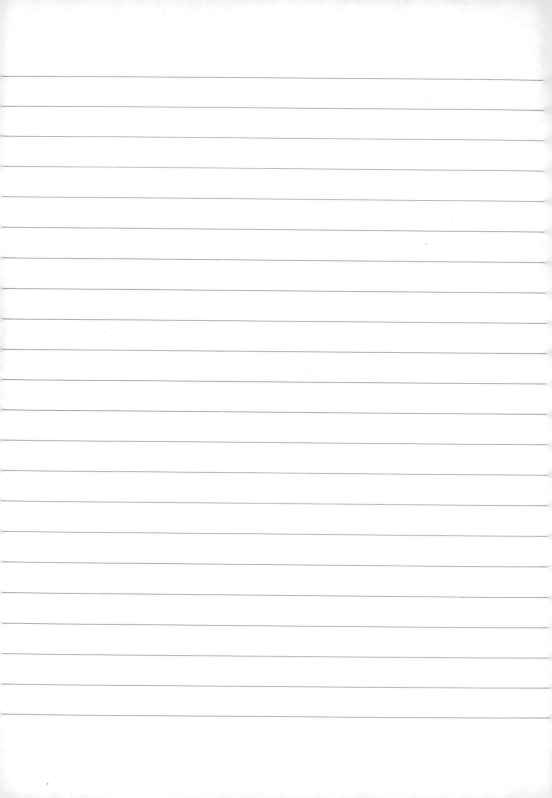

\ <u></u>				
***************************************	************	****		

		********	~~~~~	

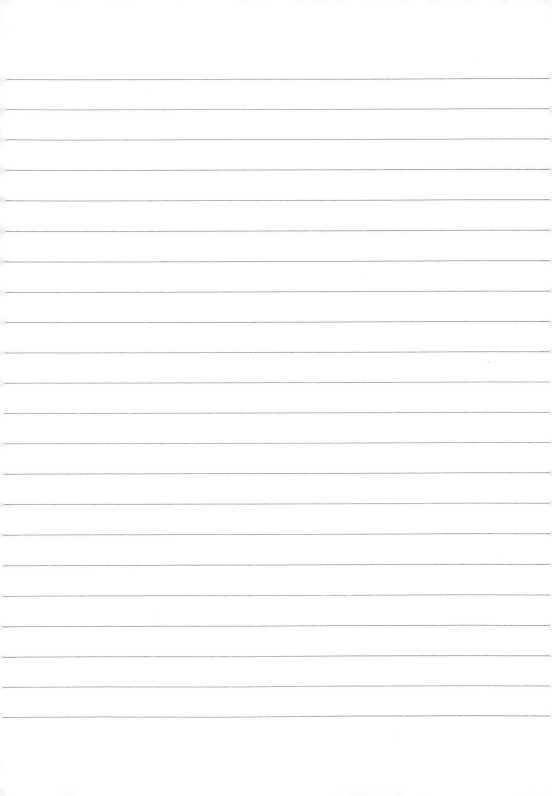

,,,,,,,,,,,,,,,,,,,,,,,,,,,,,,,,,,,,,,,					
J 					
)				******	
·					

		n.			
\				******	
J 	*****				

-			

	*****	***************************************	

)	,		
P			
		7	
·			

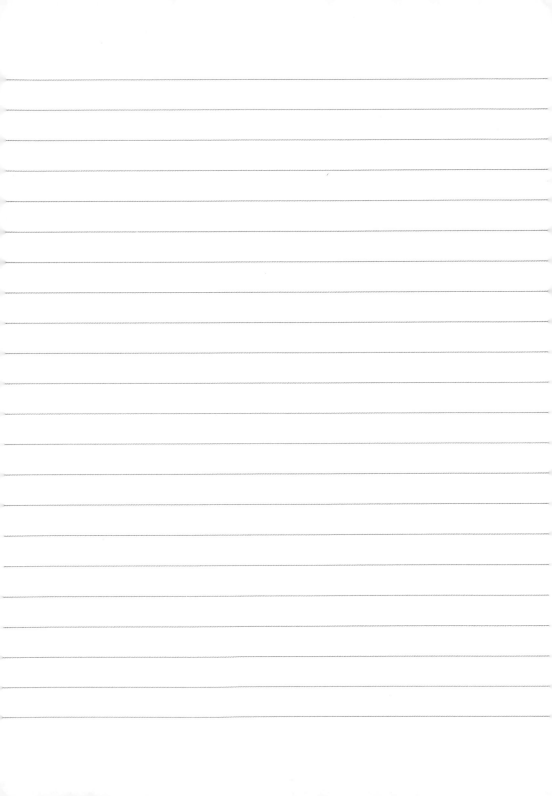

>	
·····	

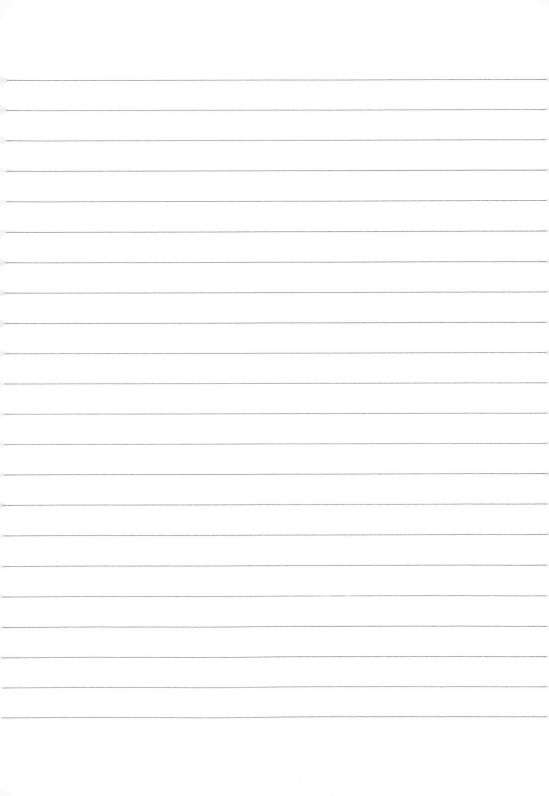

Manana and an	
·	
······································	

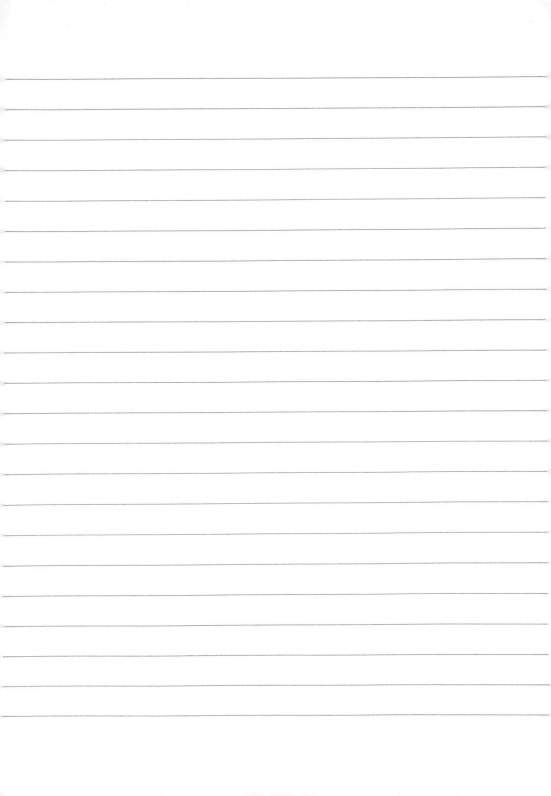

 ······

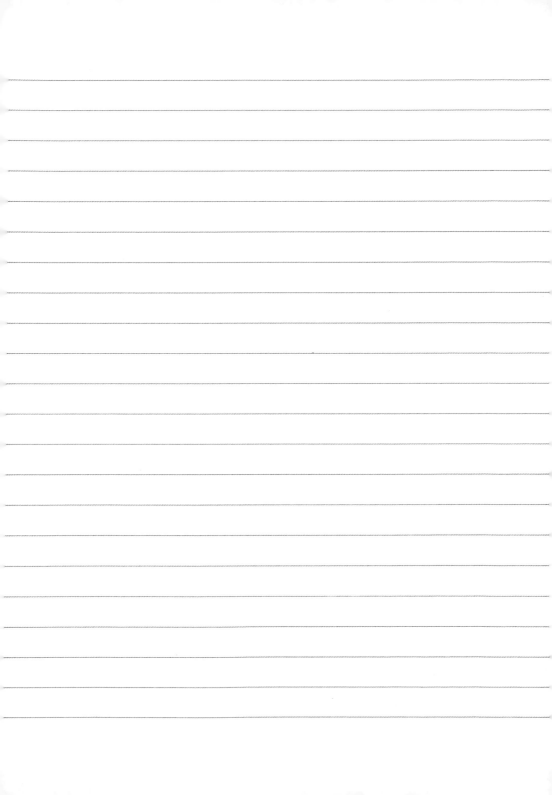

<u>}</u>	
-	


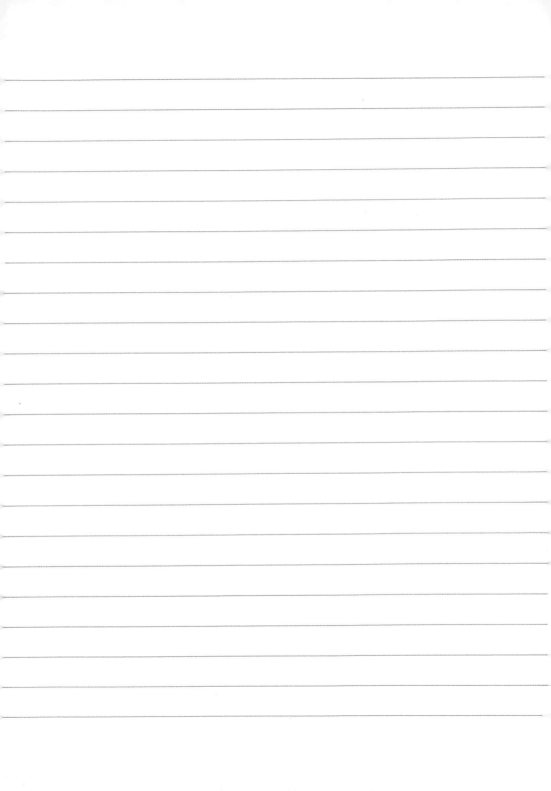

······	*****	*****		 	
)				****	

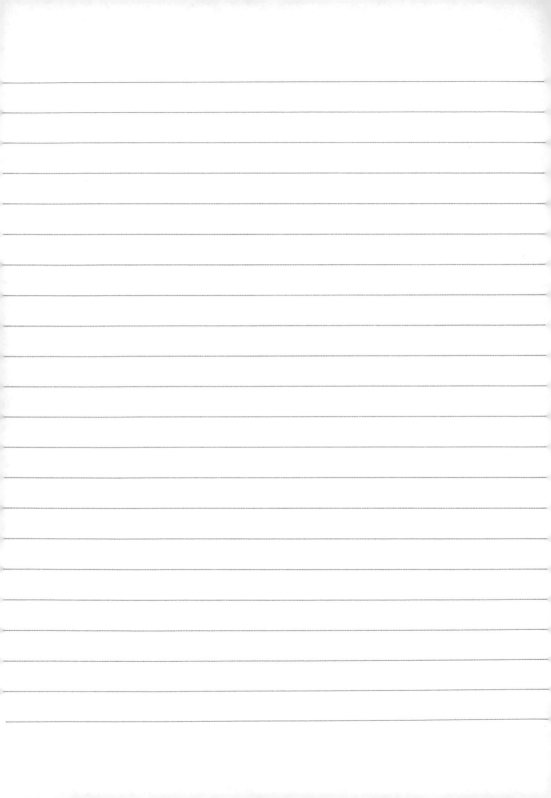

y	

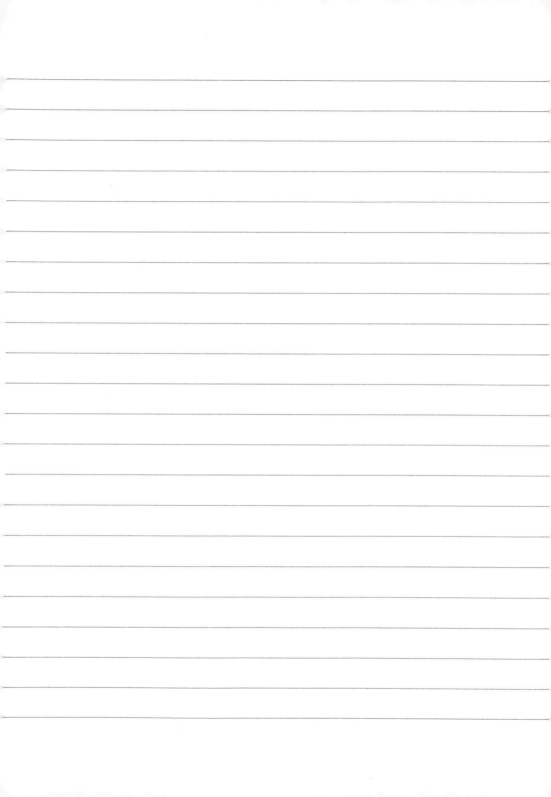

,	
jeen	
· · · · · · · · · · · · · · · · · · ·	

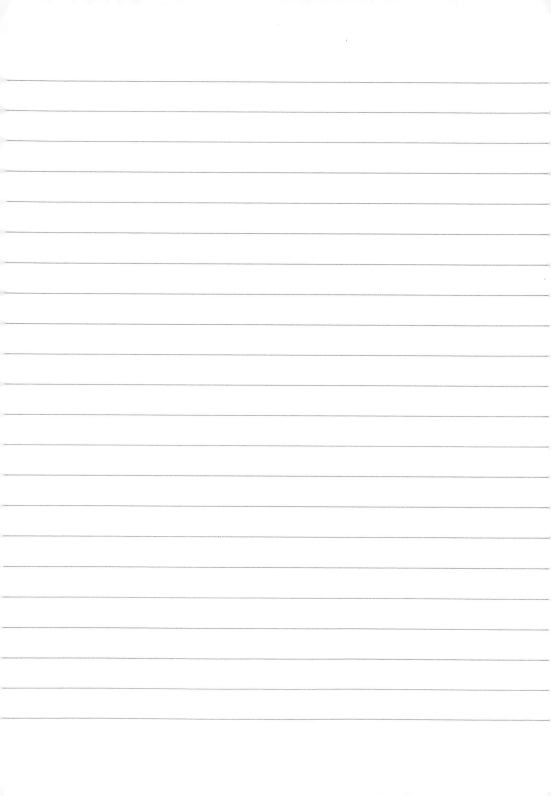

<u> </u>		 	

3 5		 	

######################################			

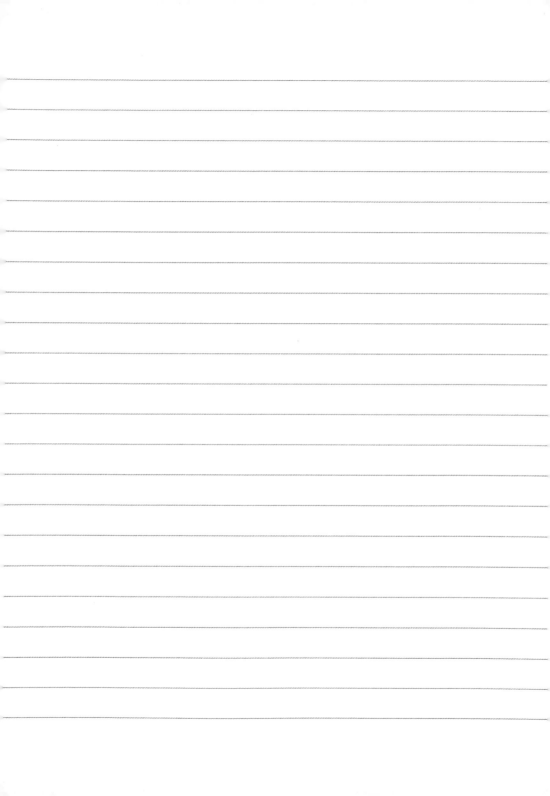

	·	
Sector contract of the sector	n	
······		

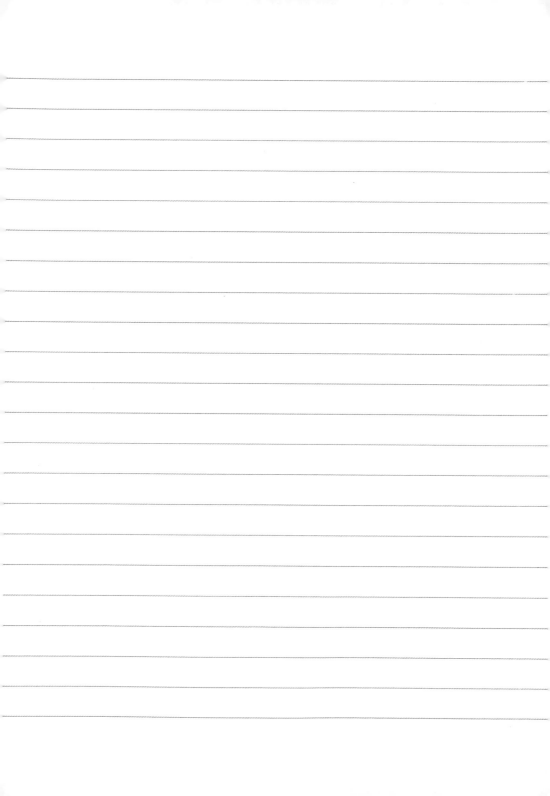

	******	******	 	 	 	
)			 	 		
			 	 	~~~~~~~~~~~~~~~~~~~~~~~~~~~~~~~~~~~~~~~	 

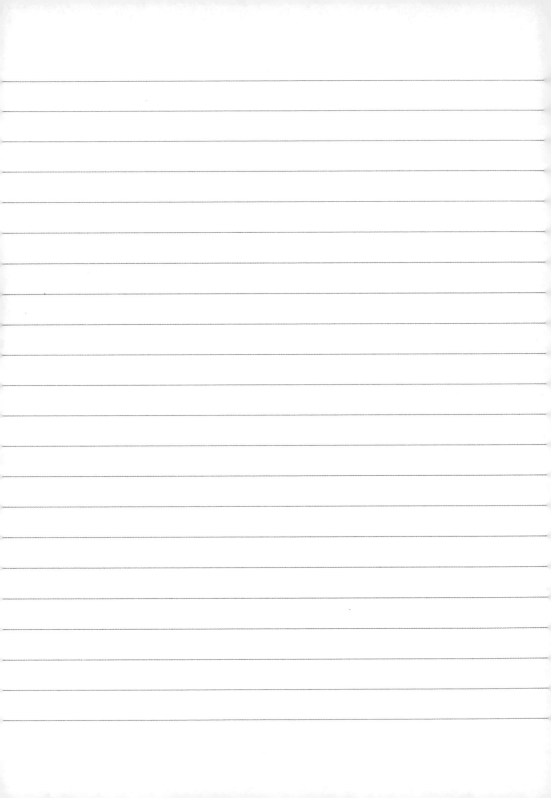

×	
·	

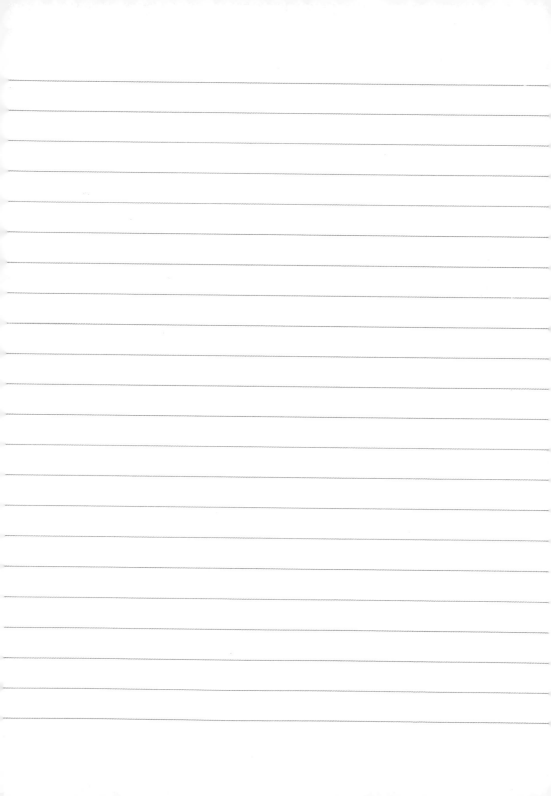

			*****		 
	********				 
				~~~~	
	3				

	******	~~~~~			
·····	~~~~~				


			~~~~~		 
			******		 
		,			
	***********				 